Guffey's

JobSearch Express

Job Hunting on the World Wide Web

Prepared by

Mary Ellen Guffey

SOUTH-WESTERN

TM

THOMSON LEARNING

Australia · Canada · Mexico · Singapore · Spair · United Kingdom · United States

JobSearch Express: Job Hunting on the World Wide Web
by Mary Ellen Guffey

Team Leader: Melissa Acuna
Acquisitions Editor: Pamela M. Person
Developmental Editor: Mary Draper
Marketing Manager: Mark Callahan
Production Editor: Kelly Keeler
Manufacturing Coordinator: Sandee Milewski
Printer: Globus Printing

Printed in the United States of America
  3 4 5 04 03 02 01

For more information contact South-Western, 5101 Madison Road, Cincinnati, Ohio, 45227 or find us on the Internet at http://www.swcollege.com

For permission to use material from this text or product,contact us by
• **telephone: 1-800-730-2214**
• **fax: 1-800-730-2215**
• **web:** http://www.thomsonrights.com

ISBN 0-324-14972-7

The Guffey JobSearch Express

Introduction

The Internet has definitely changed the way people look for jobs and send their résumés. In the past, job seekers waited for the Sunday edition of their local newspapers, scoured the classified ads, and then sent off handsome print copies of their résumés. Today, many job seekers begin with a computer search of Internet job listings. Then they fire off "plain Jane" résumés by e-mail, or they submit print copies that they expect will be scanned by a computer rather than a person.

Knowing how to use the Internet to your advantage can save you an enormous amount of time and may help you find your dream job. Although most of the traditional advice for writing résumés and searching for jobs still holds true, you should learn more about how résumés are processed today, especially by large companies.

In this *Guffey JobSearch Express*, our goal is to amplify the basic information presented in your textbook. If you will soon be looking for a job, first read the chapter in your book about employment communication. Then use this *JobSearch Express* to supplement what you learned in the textbook.

In addition to showing you how to prepare a scannable résumé, this booklet presents the author's top picks for career resources on the Internet. If you have tried using the Web to answer any employment questions, you know how confusing it can be. Thousands of career sites have popped up, and many claim to be No. 1. We have evaluated most of the best-known sites and selected our "Top Picks" in five categories: Internships, Job Search Resources, Résumé Resources, Salary Information, and Company Information. A brief profile of each site tells what we considered exceptional and what you might find useful. Additional Internet resources and hot links are provided at the Guffey Student Web site.

Preparing a Scannable Résumé

This supplement provides you with all you need to know about preparing a scannable résumé, including definitions, writing techniques, a checklist, before-and-after samples, and models for college students. To make this information easy to read, we present most of it in question-and-answer format for quick comprehension and reference.

What is a scannable résumé?

A scannable résumé is one that can be "read" electronically by an employer's optical character recognition (OCR) hardware and software. An OCR converts the characters from a printed page into text that is stored in a database. Employers then use special software to search for keywords, phrases, or skills targeted for a position. Many companies now use electronic applicant tracking systems to scan incoming résumés, create databases, and even rank candidates for positions.

What is an ASCII résumé?

An ASCII (pronounced *ask´ ee*) résumé is one that is stored in clear text format. ASCII is the simplest form of text. It includes no formatting, and the text is not platform- or application-specific. Typical styling devices (such as bolding, italicizing, and underscoring) do not show up in ASCII text. It is identified by the ".txt" file extension. Its main purpose is to send text between computers. A résumé prepared as an ASCII file will look rather plain, but it is often requested by employers because all computer systems can read it.

What is the difference between a scannable résumé and an ASCII résumé?

The primary difference between a scannable résumé and an ASCII résumé is that the former is printed on paper and must be scanned. An ASCII résumé is generally sent by e-mail and is an electronic document.

Why do some employers use scanning techniques?

Many organizations, especially larger companies, are overwhelmed by the huge number of résumés that they receive. By using scanning techniques and applicant tracking systems, organizations realize a number of advantages:

- **Enables electronic searching.** Scanning techniques enable employers to organize incoming résumés so that data can be electronically searched. If a hiring supervisor requests a person with specific experience, skills, or qualifications, that person's résumé can be easily located.

- **Reduces costs.** Fewer personnel are necessary to process incoming résumés because the new technology significantly reduces the time it takes to screen candidates.

- **Speeds hiring process.** Employers find that applicant tracking systems speed the entire hiring process, thus saving time and money. Applicants can be notified more quickly, and companies can fill their needs swiftly.

Why should I learn to write a scannable résumé?

- **To be prepared.** As many as 80 percent of today's larger organizations are using scanning devices and applicant tracking systems to process their job candidates.

- **To compete.** Remember that other job seekers will have qualifications similar to yours, and they will very likely have scannable résumés.

How do I know whether to submit a scannable résumé?

Some companies scan and others do not. One way to find out is to visit the company's Web site and look for information about job applications. Some organizations even provide advice on how to prepare your résumé for optimum effectiveness. If the company's Web site is not helpful, call the organization and ask whether it scans résumés.

What are the advantages to submitting a scannable résumé?

- **Expanded opportunities.** When you send a résumé that can be scanned, you open up multiple job possibilities. You may be considered for positions you didn't even know were available. When your résumé becomes part of a company's database, it is available for jobs in all departments of the organization.

- **Faster processing.** Since applicant tracking systems work faster than people, employers are able to get the results of their decisions to you sooner. This means that you spend less time waiting for responses.

- **Reduced bias.** Scanned résumés can reduce exclusion resulting from bias in the selection process. Computers, unlike humans, make decisions objectively; they carry no preconceptions.

- **Longer shelf life.** Information from résumés that have been electronically scanned is available for an extended period of time. Without additional effort from you, your résumé may remain active for years.

What are the disadvantages to submitting a scannable résumé?

- **Mechanical selection.** It's frightening to think that a computer is making all initial selection choices. As we all know, machines make mistakes.

- **Ineffective keywords.** If you did not include just the right keywords, your résumé may not be selected.

- **Less negotiation possible.** If you listed a salary range or if your past salary was high, your résumé may be excluded—even though you might be willing to negotiate a lower starting salary.

- **Difficult to update.** If your résumé languishes in a database for a long time, it may become outdated and not reflect your most recent qualifications.

How is a scannable résumé different from a traditional résumé?

Writers of traditional résumés are encouraged to focus on action verbs (such as *coordinated, evaluated, presented,* and *performed*). But most employers sort incoming résumés with nouns (such as *supervisor, manager, B.S.*). Thus, scannable résumés should focus on nouns. However, it's rather difficult to write a coherent résumé without verbs. Our advice is to use both action verbs and nouns, but be sure you include the keywords from your profession. A scannable résumé also differs from a traditional résumé in its appearance.

It avoids graphics and any characters not found on a standard keyboard. Another difference involves length. Although experts generally suggest that traditional résumés be limited to one page, scannable résumés can be longer.

What are some basic format and print guidelines for preparing a scannable résumé?

- List your name at the top of every page of your résumé.
- Provide your contact information (address, city/state/zip, telephone, e-mail) on separate lines on the first page.
- Don't fold or staple your résumé.
- Avoid columns, graphics, and shading.
- Don't use headers or footers.
- Avoid italics and bolding, especially in combination.
- Use sans serif fonts such as Univers, Arial, or Helvetica in 12- to 14-point size. Don't use Times Roman 10 point. Your goal is to avoid letters that touch each other.
- Substitute asterisks for bullets.
- Don't use boxes or horizontal or vertical lines.
- Use capital letters to distinguish section headings.
- Print on white paper with a laser jet printer so that you can send clean, crisp copies.

How can I use keywords most effectively?

When a scanner recognizes a keyword in your résumé, it's called a "hit." Your résumé is ranked according to the number of keyword hits. Only résumés with the targeted keywords will be selected for review. To improve the number of hits in your résumé, use keywords and skill-focused words that apply to your career. Substitute descriptive nouns and skills for vague language. You'll want to focus on the following kinds of keywords:

- **Job titles.** Include a number of job titles that describe the position you seek. For example, *Personal computer support specialist, PC trainer, PC trouble-shooter, Software support.*

- **Skills and responsibilities.** Study job postings in your field to learn what employers seek. For example, a nursing candidate might list *Acute care, Code 99, catheter care, infusion therapy, five years' experience.*

- **Acronyms and industry terminology.** Be familiar with the jargon of your profession. What abbreviations might an employer use for a job description in your field? A Web designer might list terms such as *Flash, DHTML, Jscript, CSS, Photoshop.*

- **Education or certification.** Include specifics such as *Certified Network Administrator, CNA, BS in Computer Science, Certified Public Accountant, CPA.*

A good way to identify keywords is to underline all skills listed in employment ads or job descriptions for the types of jobs that you want. Generally, you'll focus on nouns. However, verbs such as *troubleshoot* or *calibrate* may also be used to identify some positions.

What is a keyword summary and should I use one?

A keyword summary is a paragraph listing all the relevant keywords you can find for the position you want. It may be placed after your job name, after your job objective, or at the end of your résumé. Is it mandatory? No. If you have been careful in using keywords throughout your résumé, you can skip a keyword summary. Remember, though, that the more keywords you have, the greater your chances of ranking high. Some job candidates use *Summary of Qualifications* instead of a keyword summary. It highlights a candidate's experience and most significant qualifications. It also includes many keywords.

Will my scannable résumé look uninteresting?

Although scannable résumés are simple, they can also be attractive. Strive to use white space carefully. Use capital letters for headings. Most scanners will also read bold print, although they have trouble with bold/italic combinations. Some experts suggest sending two résumés, one for scanning and one for human eyes. Other experts say that sending two résumés is confusing to the receiving organization. It's probably best to call in advance and ask.

Should I worry about scanning if I'm sending my résumé by e-mail?

Some companies with advanced equipment may be able to transfer a résumé from an e-mail system into a résumé-tracking system. Other organizations might print your résumé from e-mail and then scan it into the system. To be safe, if you send a résumé as an attachment to an e-mail message, be sure that your résumé has been saved as an ASCII file.

Should I follow up after submitting my résumé?

Employment expert and author Joyce Lain Kennedy recommends following up with a telephone call three or four days after submitting your résumé to a company that you know uses an applicant tracking system. If possible, learn the name of the administrator or operator/verifier. Ask that person these questions: "Did you receive my résumé? Was I a match anywhere? Has my résumé been routed? To whom? Which department?" The key word here is "routed." Using this word suggests that you have taken the time to learn about the hiring process. Although you may get "stonewalled" when you call, you lose nothing if your manner is tactful and professional.

Checklist for Writing an Effective Scannable Résumé

In addition to the suggestions in your textbook for writing a persuasive résumé, follow these tips to make your résumé scannable:

✓ **Place your name first.** Be sure it stands on a line by itself and that none of the letters overlap. If your name is misread by the scanner, your résumé may be lost forever.

✓ **Use separate lines for contact information.** Put your address, telephone number, and e-mail address on separate lines.

✓ **Avoid fancy formatting.** Don't use columns, graphics, shading, headers, footers, italics, boxes, or horizontal or vertical lines.

✓ **Keep it flat.** Use a large envelope so that you can send it without folding.

✓ **Use simple formatting techniques.** Put headings in capital letters and use hyphens or asterisks in place of bullets. Provide ample white space to improve readability.

✓ **Use Arial, Univers, or Helvetica font.** These san serifs fonts are easiest for scanners to read. Strive for 12- to 14-point font size.

✓ **Produce clean copy.** Use a laser jet printer and white paper. Don't send copies that have been faxed or made by a copier.

✓ **Focus on keywords.** Include job titles, skills, responsibilities, acronyms and industry terminology, and education and certifications. Select nouns that are used to describe the job you want.

✓ **Don't limit yourself to one page.** Because scanned résumés can be longer, don't hesitate to use two pages if necessary.

✓ **Consider sending an ASCII file.** If you are sending your résumé by e-mail, you should probably prepare it as a plain text (ASCII) file.

✓ **Follow up with a phone call.** Three or four days after submitting your scannable résumé, check to see whether it was entered into the system and was routed to any departments.

Before-and-After Résumé

Figure 1 is a typical résumé of a recent college graduate. Not only is it poorly formatted for scanning, but it also does not promote relevant skills and experience for the position desired.

The "before" version of Carolyn's résumé has a number of formatting faults that would make it difficult to scan. Her name should appear on a line by itself without graphics. Each line of her contact information should be separate. She should not use italics, and she should use a simple font, such as Arial. The two-column layout might also cause problems. In addition to these formatting faults, this résumé does a poor job of selling Carolyn's skills and experience for the position she wants.

The version in **Figure 2** adds more information, formats it for easy scanning, and highlights Carolyn's qualifications for the public relations position she seeks. This improved version includes many keywords related to the field of public relations.

FIGURE 1 Before

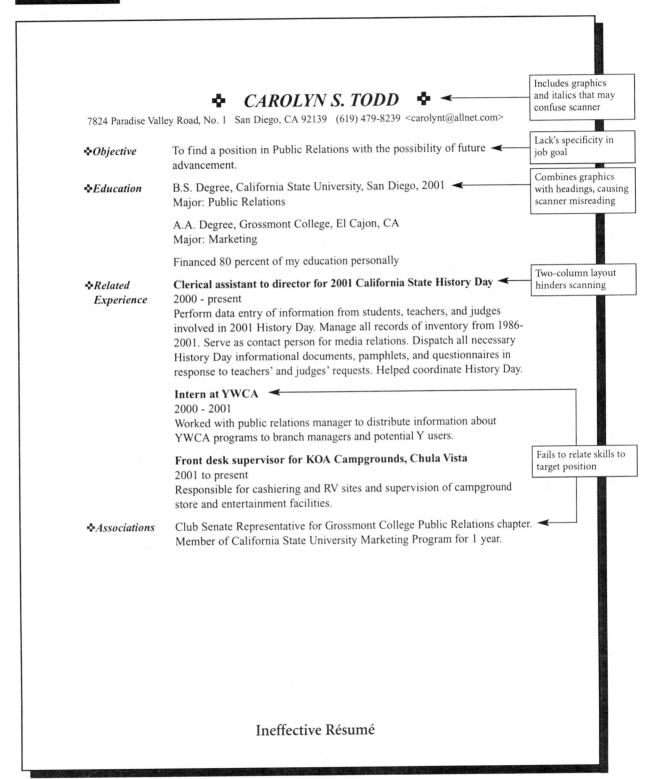

✠ *CAROLYN S. TODD* ✠

7824 Paradise Valley Road, No. 1   San Diego, CA 92139   (619) 479-8239   <carolynt@allnet.com>

Includes graphics and italics that may confuse scanner

✠*Objective*   To find a position in Public Relations with the possibility of future advancement.

Lack's specificity in job goal

✠*Education*   B.S. Degree, California State University, San Diego, 2001
Major: Public Relations

Combines graphics with headings, causing scanner misreading

A.A. Degree, Grossmont College, El Cajon, CA
Major: Marketing

Financed 80 percent of my education personally

✠*Related Experience*   **Clerical assistant to director for 2001 California State History Day**
2000 - present
Perform data entry of information from students, teachers, and judges involved in 2001 History Day. Manage all records of inventory from 1986-2001. Serve as contact person for media relations. Dispatch all necessary History Day informational documents, pamphlets, and questionnaires in response to teachers' and judges' requests. Helped coordinate History Day.

Two-column layout hinders scanning

Intern at YWCA
2000 - 2001
Worked with public relations manager to distribute information about YWCA programs to branch managers and potential Y users.

Front desk supervisor for KOA Campgrounds, Chula Vista
2001 to present
Responsible for cashiering and RV sites and supervision of campground store and entertainment facilities.

Fails to relate skills to target position

✠*Associations*   Club Senate Representative for Grossmont College Public Relations chapter. Member of California State University Marketing Program for 1 year.

Ineffective Résumé

FIGURE 2 After

CAROLYN S. TODD ◄——————————————— | Places name first; uses Arial font |

7824 Paradise Valley Road, No. 1
San Diego, CA 92129 ◄——————————— | Provides separate lines for key items |
(619) 479-8239
<carolynt@allnet.com>

| Uses many keywords related to target position |

OBJECTIVE

Public relations position using my experience in media relations, press release development, writing of community news stories, events coordination, supervision, and leadership of public relations and marketing associations.

MEDIA RELATIONS ◄——————————— | Groups experience into key skill categories |

Assistant to director, 2001 California State History Day, 2000 to present

* Served as liaison to newspapers, radio stations, and television stations to promote California State History Day.

* Prepared and issued press releases over a three-month period to 36 media organizations resulting in publicity in the California Reporter (circulation 150,000), California State University, San Diego, campus newspaper (circulation 20,000), ten community service television spots (audience of 60,000), and six 32-second radio spots (audience 45,000). ◄

* Gained public event coordination skill by assisting Dean of History Program in creation, production, and distribution of 10,000 pieces of collateral PR materials. Coordinated events scheduling and management for 1,200 attendees of the History Day event.

| Lists spefcific, quantifiable achievements; includes many keywords |

PUBLIC RELATIONS

Intern. Assistant to Public Relations Director
San Diego YWCA
2000 - 2001

* Prepared press releases distributed to 12 branch locations, radio, TV, and newspapers working directly with the public relations manager for district serving a population of 12,000 women and children. Completed a six-month internship program, receiving an excellent rating from the public relations manager. ◄

* Communicated with staff of 24 branch managers and events coordinators to write news stories for over 200 events with total attendance of 30,000. Previewed stories with public relations manager, being complimented on thoroughness and writing skill with few stories needing any editing. Coordinated release of stories with public relations manager. ◄

| Relates achievements to target position |

Effective Résumé

FIGURE 2 After (continued)

CAROLYN S. TODD
page 2

CUSTOMER SERVICE MANAGEMENT

Uses vocabulary of target position to describe experience

Supervisor
KOA Campgrounds, Chula Vista
2001 to present

* Manage customer service, front desk, and accommodations scheduling for up to 600 customers per week.

* Account for up to $20,000 in cash monthly.

* Trained and supervised two assistants working part-time in all areas of customer service, cashiering, scheduling, and completion of accounting records.

LEADERSHIP TRAINING

Emphasizes skills that employers seek

* Club Senate Representative, Grossmont College Public Relations Chapter, 1996-1998. Served as mentor to 30 students planning to transfer to California State University and major in public relations. Led membership meetings for groups of up to 50 and promoted meetings by creating and distributing public relations notices.

* Marketing Program Chairperson, California State University Marketing Association, 2000. Developed five instructive marketing programs for groups of up to 50 students.

Model Scannable Résumés

Figures 3–5 illustrate more versions of scannable résumés. **Model 1** (**Figure 3**) describes a candidate with several years of experience. It uses a keyword summary at the beginning. **Model 2** (**Figure 4**) shows the résumé of a student about to receive a two-year degree. It begins with a "Summary of Qualifications" section, which many employers appreciate. **Model 3** (**Figure 5**) describes a candidate with a two-year degree who is seeking a position in office administration. Her résumé includes a keyword summary, but the résumé would be more effective if she described her experience more fully and in terms of how it would benefit a future employer.

FIGURE **3** Model 1

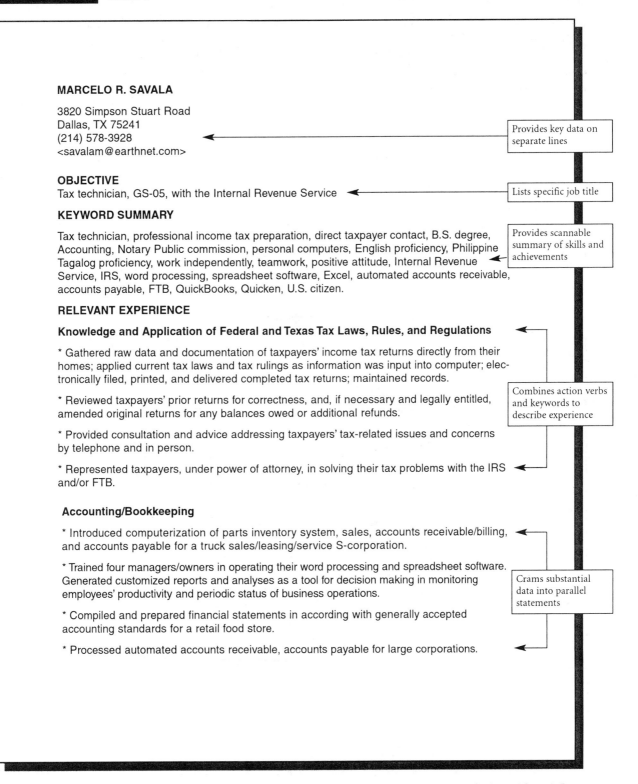

MARCELO R. SAVALA

3820 Simpson Stuart Road
Dallas, TX 75241
(214) 578-3928
<savalam@earthnet.com>

Provides key data on
separate lines

OBJECTIVE
Tax technician, GS-05, with the Internal Revenue Service

Lists specific job title

KEYWORD SUMMARY

Tax technician, professional income tax preparation, direct taxpayer contact, B.S. degree, Accounting, Notary Public commission, personal computers, English proficiency, Philippine Tagalog proficiency, work independently, teamwork, positive attitude, Internal Revenue Service, IRS, word processing, spreadsheet software, Excel, automated accounts receivable, accounts payable, FTB, QuickBooks, Quicken, U.S. citizen.

Provides scannable
summary of skills and
achievements

RELEVANT EXPERIENCE

Knowledge and Application of Federal and Texas Tax Laws, Rules, and Regulations

* Gathered raw data and documentation of taxpayers' income tax returns directly from their homes; applied current tax laws and tax rulings as information was input into computer; electronically filed, printed, and delivered completed tax returns; maintained records.

* Reviewed taxpayers' prior returns for correctness, and, if necessary and legally entitled, amended original returns for any balances owed or additional refunds.

* Provided consultation and advice addressing taxpayers' tax-related issues and concerns by telephone and in person.

* Represented taxpayers, under power of attorney, in solving their tax problems with the IRS and/or FTB.

Combines action verbs
and keywords to
describe experience

Accounting/Bookkeeping

* Introduced computerization of parts inventory system, sales, accounts receivable/billing, and accounts payable for a truck sales/leasing/service S-corporation.

* Trained four managers/owners in operating their word processing and spreadsheet software. Generated customized reports and analyses as a tool for decision making in monitoring employees' productivity and periodic status of business operations.

* Compiled and prepared financial statements in according with generally accepted accounting standards for a retail food store.

* Processed automated accounts receivable, accounts payable for large corporations.

Crams substantial
data into parallel
statements

The Guffey JobSearch Express

FIGURE 3 Model 1 (continued)

MARCELO R. SAVALA
page 2

> Uses second page to
> fully document
> experience and skills

Notary Public Service

* Served as official of State of Texas in detection and deterrence of fraudulent public records.

* Served the general public in making lawful and reasonable requests, notarizing documents, taking acknowledgements, administering oaths and affirmations, and performing other acts authorized by law.

COMMUNITY SERVICE

* Volunteered for the IRS/FTB VITA program during eight tax seasons. Helped low-income taxpayers prepare their federal and state tax returns; answered questions related to latest tax law and changes.

* Served as pro bono volunteer and income tax counselor for eight consecutive tax seasons in the Texas Tax Counseling for the Elderly program for taxpayers aged 60 and older.

WORK HISTORY

> Shows quick summary
> of work and activities

1998 to present. Tax preparer, notary public. Self-employed, Grand Prairie, Texas.
1995-1998. Accounting temp, Accountants, Inc., Dallas, Texas.
1995-1996. Traveled worldwide.
1993-1995. Student, Stephen F. Austin State University, Nacogdoches, Texas.
1991-1993. Data entry operator, Planning Department, City of Dallas.

EDUCATION AND CREDENTIALS

* B.S., Stephen F. Austin State University, 1995. GPA: 3.57; Major GPA: 3.62
* 1040 Running Start, ISTC, 1998; Electronic Filing Roundtable
* Registered Tax Preparer, current certification, State of Texas
* Notary Public, current certification, State of Texas

FIGURE 4 Model 2

TREVOR H. JOHNSON

1214 Springdale Road
Decatur, GA 30625
(240) 466-8724
<thjohnson@aol.com>

OBJECTIVE

Challenging position in management within a professional organization leading to a position as an executive administrator.

SUMMARY OF QUALIFICATIONS ◄————————————————————— Spotlights key qualifications up front

Education: DeKalb College, A.A. degree expected 6/02

Experience: Office manager for roofing firm for 2 1/2 years; additional experience as assistant manager in drug store.

Strengths: Communication skills, organization, leadership, ambition, word processing, Excel

EDUCATION ◄————————————————————————————— Places education first because it's probably more important than experience

DeKalb College, Decatur, GA. Associate of Arts degree expected 6/02. GPA: 3.2 (A = 4) Major: Business management. Minor: Computer applications.

EXPERIENCE

Office Manager, Sutton Roofing, Decatur. 8/99 to present.

* Managed the administrative office of a roofing company, including hiring, training, and supervising two employees.

* Maintained inventory with responsibility for up to $12,000 supply budget. ◄——— Quantifies experience for maximum impact

* Organized accounts payable and accounts receivable files for nearly 200 customers; mailed monthly billing statements in a timely manner.

* Answered professionally up to 100 telephone calls daily.

* Commended for organization, enthusiasm, professional work habits, and attitude.

Second Assistant Manager, Thrifty Drug Stores, Decatur, GA, 10/98 - 7/99 ◄——— Emphasizes management experience

* Managed sales floor with up to six employees.

* Made change for all cashiers; made all bank deposits.

* Handled customer complaints with success.

* Hired and trained new employees.

* Initiated new work procedures to improve sales and boost employee morale.

STRENGTHS

* Superior communication skills, both oral and written, as developed in class and on the job.

* Personal computer skills, including Microsoft Word, Excel, and PowerPoint.

* Ability to produce results and motivate others as evidenced in supervision of employees and in coaching of a successful Little League baseball team.

FIGURE 5 Model 3

ASHLEY ANN ANDERSON
1549 South Mountain Avenue
Phoenix, AZ 86030
E-mail: aaanderson@netcom.com>

OBJECTIVE ◄

Provides general
objective to qualify for
many positions

Responsible and challenging position using and amplifying my experience in administrative
office support, with opportunities to work with others as well as apply my leadership and
problem-solving skills.

KEYWORDS ◄

Lists words that
might appear in job
description

Office administration, administrative assistant, executive assistant, filing, word processing,
database management, training, supervision, Web design, Word, WordPerfect, Excel,
PowerPoint, Microsoft Money, QuarkXPress, PageMaker, Photoshop, PageMill, Illustrator,
Freehand, Netscape Navigator, Microsoft Outlook.

EDUCATION

* Gateway Community College, Phoenix, Arizona. A.A. degree in office management, 2001.
GPA: 3.81 (4 = A).

* Uplink Computer Training Center, Phoenix, Arizona. Courses in Windows, Web design, and
desktop publishing.

SKILLS AND ABILITIES ◄

Emphasizes skills
because she has little
experience

* Extensive leadership and organizational experience as a national and state officer of Phi
Beta Lambda, business service organization, and various other volunteer activities.

* Proficient in both Macintosh and PC computer environments, using a variety of programs.

* Skilled at graphic design, word processing, and desktop publishing.

* Experienced in basic Web site design, management, and maintenance.

* Office skills include keyboarding at 90+ words a minute, filing, copying, scheduling, data
entry, faxing, answering phones, and customer support.

ACTIVITIES

* Workshop co-presenter at Elizabeth Hart Literacy Council Reading Conference, 2000.

* Chair, Judges Committee for Annual Business Skills Day, 1999. ◄

Describes activities
that suggest initiative,
leadership, and
organization

* Developed basic Web site for Phi Beta Lambda.

Career Resources on the Web: Guffey's Top Picks

Nearly everyone looking for a job today starts with the Web. Using the Web to locate a job or an internship has distinct advantages. For many job seekers, the Web leads to bigger salaries, wider opportunities, and faster hiring. The Web, however, can devour huge chunks of time and produce slim results unless you know what you are doing. In terms of actually finding a job, the Web seems to work best for professionals looking for similar work in their current fields and for those who are totally flexible about location. Yet the Web is an excellent place for any job seeker to learn what's available, what qualifications are necessary, and what salaries are being offered. Even if you don't find a job on the Web, you can learn a great deal about the entire employment process by spending some time searching Web sites.

The best-known job-related Internet resources are the job banks that provide online listings of employment openings (such as Monster.com). Many of these "electronic classifieds," however, require a significant amount of time and energy to review. The best sites allow you to enter specific parameters and receive individualized e-mail listings of corresponding positions available. In addition to job sites, you can find openings and valuable tips by visiting the Web sites of individual companies.

In this *JobSearch Express* booklet, we will give you a short list of some of the best career resources we have located at this writing. Bear in mind, though, that the Web is a rapidly changing entity. Web sites merge, disappear, expand, or suddenly change their focus. At the Guffey Student Web site <**http://www.meguffey.com**> (and its mirror site <**http://www.westwords.com/guffey/students.html**>), we strive to keep our career resource links up to date. Printed here is a short list of the best sites available. Check our Web sites for links to these sites as well as for additional links and updates.

Internships

Surprisingly, internships are increasingly becoming the route taken by job seekers to gain initial access into a company. Many organizations promote internships because they attract top talent and help organizations staff their needs. Internships also enable organizations to assess potential employees before making a job offer. Students value internships because they can learn new skills, enhance their résumés, and "try out" a company before committing to it. Listed here are some of the top Web internship sites. Another place to locate internships is at company Web sites.

InternshipPrograms.com <**http://internships.wetfeet.com/home.asp**>. Claims to be the "largest internship community on the Internet." In 2001 became a part of WebFeet.com, a comprehensive career planning and recruitment site. Must register to use database, but it's free. Search by location, career category, or company name. Offers résumé advice and articles such as "Defining Your Internship Goals," "How to Get the Internship You Want," "Internship Compensation: What to Expect," and "The Truth About Consulting Internships."

InternWeb.com <**http://www.internweb.com**>. Allows free searches by career area (marketing, communications, etc.), by employer type (business service, nonprofit, etc.), or by state. Also provides information on virtual internships (you don't have to be present). Offers articles such as "Top Five Strategies for Making the Most of Your Internship." Does not require registration, so you will not be receiving unwanted e-mail.

RisingStar Internships <http://www.rsinternships.com>. Provides database of national internships openings for students. Search by sector (accounting, business, etc.). Prospective interns may post their résumés on the site. Not an extensive database of openings, but gives a quick overview of internship possibilities.

Job Search Resources

Formerly, job seekers would begin their search with the newspaper classified ads. Today, they can find many of those ads online, either at the newspapers' own Web sites or at hundreds of specialized Web sites devoted to job listings. Over 2,000 Web sites now specialize in job listings (*Monthly Labor Review*, 2001). Shown here are some of the best-known employment sites. You can find links to these and to other job sites at the Guffey Web site. When you visit these sites, take advantage of the amazing collection of informative articles, columns, and forums that many sites offer. In addition to job listings, most of them provide terrific free career advice devoted to such topics as getting hired, negotiating offers, working life, getting ahead on the job, work and family, and workplace transitions. It's free! Take advantage of it.

Monster.com <http://www.monster.com>. Provides access to information on more than 500,000 job opportunities. Publishes 11 free career newsletters that are currently subscribed to by more than 400,000 readers. Allows users to search 3,000 pages of career advice, résumés, company information, and salary data. Search for jobs by job category, city, or nation. Considered by many to be the premier Web job site.

WetFeet.com <http://www.wetfeet.com>. Requires registration (which means you may receive unwanted e-mail), but it's free. In addition to extensive job listings, offers "expert advice on everything from résumés to getting dressed." Features exclusive company interviews and a searchable database of thousands of company profiles so that you can learn about a company before applying. Definitely worth a visit.

CareerBuilder <http://www.careerbuilder.com>. Joined forces with media giants to offer "industry's most targeted online network of career centers." Job seekers have access to *Los Angeles Times*, *Chicago Tribune*, and other newspapers' classified ads as well as job opportunities posted by 654 employers. Visitors can register for personal search agents and may seek advice from career industry experts. Searches can be tailored with specific criteria at 75 + job sites.

College Grad Job Hunter <http://www.collegegrad.com>. Furnishes information about résumé creation, cover letters, interviewing, salary negotiation, etc. Offers information on "entry level job opportunities for college students and recent grads," as well as on "Positions requiring one or more years work experience." Maintains an on-line career forum managed by Brian Krueger, author of the book *College Grad Job Hunter: Insider Techniques and Tactics for Finding a Top-Paying Entry Level Job*.

Résumé Resources

Although you receive lots of information about writing résumés in your textbook and in this guide, you may want to see what experts on the Web have to say about writing résumés. Some sites provide savvy advice and even offer samples. Here are a few sites that we consider the best. Remember, these and other hot links are available at the Guffey Web site.

Writing a Résumé—Career Development Center <http://www.mtholyoke.edu/offices/careers/handouts/resume.htm>. Sponsored by the Mt. Holyoke Career Development Center, this site discusses format, planning, content, action words, layout, guidelines, and electronic résumés. It also provides sample résumés.

The Damn Good Résumé <http://www.damngood.com>. Yana Parker—author of *Damn Good Résumé Guide; Résumé Catalog: 200 Damn Good Examples; Blue Collar & Beyond: Résumés for Skilled Trades & Services; Résumé Pro: Make Money Writing Résumés; Ready-to-Go Résumés*, and other books—offers lively and informative pages with titles such as "20 Hot Tips on Résumés," 52 Job-Search Q & A's," and "25 Tough Résumé Problems."

Résumé Tutor <http://www1.umn.edu/ohr/ecep/resume/>. Provides an interactive workbook created by the University of Minnesota Office of Human Resources. Takes you through a six-step résumé-creation process.

JobStar—Résumés <http://jobstar.org/tools/resume/index.htm>. Explains résumés, discusses four résumé types, shows samples, describes electronic résumé banks, and provides expert tips.

Salary Information

One of the most troubling aspects of finding a job is deciding what salary range to name. If you guess too low, you may undersell your talents. If you guess too high, you may never even get an interview. A number of Web sites provide advice on what salaries to expect in various job categories in different parts of the country. The following top picks offer reliable wage data.

Salary.com <http://www.salary.com>. Provides salary news, advice, talk, and wizard. Also offers salary negotiation tips. Salary wizard contains salary information on thousands of job titles. It calculates salaries based on job title and geographic location.

JobStar <http://www.jobsmart.org>. Offers links to general salary surveys as well as links to profession-specific salary surveys. Although JobStar's career database is oriented toward California job seekers, its comprehensive information is used by people throughout the United States.

Wall Street Journal's "CareerJournal" <http://www.careerjournal.com/default.asp>. Site offers links to salary data and salary-oriented articles for "thousands of positions." Click on "Salary and Hiring Info."

Company Information

Where can you learn more about a targeted industry or a specific company where you might want to work? The best approach is to go to the company's Web site and search it thoroughly. To find the Web site addresses of many American and international companies, you can use Hoovers Online (listed below) or you can put the company name into a search engine such as Google <http://www.google.com>. In addition, you should check special Web sites devoted to company and industry news. We list here three excellent sources of company information enabling you to compare companies, check products and latest news, and examine financials. Such information helps you decide whether you want to apply to a company and also enables you to learn inside information so that you can ace an employment interview.

Hoovers Online <http://www.hoovers.com>. Offers company capsules on 14,000 public and private enterprises in the United States and around the world. Provides basic company and financial information, as well as hot links to company Web sites.

WetFeet.com <http://www.wetfeet.com/research/companies.asp>. Enables you to read 1,600 snapshots of companies including their history, business, profitability, and jobs.

Monster.com <http://company.monster.com>. Provides industry news in many categories and executive summaries of articles. Links to more detailed company data and competitive intelligence information. Click "Career Center," look for "Industries and Professions."